YOUR BOOK MATTERS

HOW TO SUCCESSFULLY WRITE AND PUBLISH YOUR BOOK

Rebecca Simmons

Diligence Publishing Company
Bloomfield, New Jersey

YOUR BOOK MATTERS
HOW TO SUCCESSFULLY WRITE AND
PUBLISH YOUR BOOK

YOUR BOOK MATTERS
HOW TO SUCCESSFULLY WRITE AND
PUBLISH YOUR BOOK

To contact Rebecca Simmons to give a publishing
workshop or speak at your organization, email:
rebeccaempowers@gmail.com

Printed in the United States

TABLE OF CONTENTS

CHAPTER ONE

WELCOME TO THE WORLD OF WRITING

You have a book inside of you, and your book matters. It's time to write your book! You have a story to tell, expertise to share, wisdom and motivation to be imparted so that someone else can be encouraged, educated, or inspired. Your book needs to be written and published because someone needs to read it.

You have probably been thinking about writing a book for some time now, and every time you hear that someone has just written a new book, your heart probably skips a beat. You wish that you could write a book and have it published, and you wonder how that person did it.

Well, if that's true, I am here to help you write your book! I once felt the same way, and I did it. I wrote and published not only one book, but twelve books. I have personally coached many other authors through the process of writing and publishing their books through my publishing company, Diligence Publishing Company, and my *"Write Your Book Fast Program"* and *"Write Your Book In 30 Days Bootcamp."*

After reading this manual, you will be more equipped to write and publish that book that you have always wanted to write. I am so excited about sharing this information with you! I am confident that this book will help you to release and birth out the book or books that you have stored up on the inside of you. I believe that after reading this book, you will be motivated to finish writing your book and to get it published.

Your book must be written! It is a part of your purpose here on earth. Too many people have left this earth with untold stories, unwritten books, unfulfilled purpose, and unlived dreams. That is why I'm encouraging you to take this manual and use it to help you to tell your story, to write your book, and ultimately to live your dreams of becoming a published author.

First, you will need to identify what type of book you want to write and why you want to write it. Like any objective in life, writing a book takes what I call GFA (Goals, Focus, and Activity). Turn the page and let's get started!

Power Point 1:

*Like any objective in life,
writing a book takes what I call GFA
(Goals, Focus, and Activity).*

CHAPTER TWO

GOALS (FOR WRITING YOUR BOOK)

Before we go any further, I recommend that you get a writer's notebook or journal. This will be used for the exercises that I will give you to do and to write down the answers to the questions that will be asked as you prepare to write your book. You can also use this book as your own personal writer's workbook and jot your answers to the questions in the space provided. Now let's dig in.

You need to know the type of book that you want to write. Do you want to write a fiction novel, or are you more inclined to write a self-help or a how-to book? Perhaps you would like to write a book about a social issue that is close to your heart. Do you have a burning desire to write a book about your own life, or perhaps to document the life of one of your relatives who has made a substantial impact on your life or in society?

You will also need to identify what do you hope to achieve by writing a book. Have you always wanted to write a book? Is it to gain fame, to leave a legacy, to tell your story, or to help people?

What qualifies you to write such a book? Is it your education, your work experience, or is it your life experiences in relationships, parenting, or mentoring?

When do you want your book to be released? Do you have a target date in mind for your book release party or launch? Are you writing for an upcoming conference? Is your material relative to something that's going on today, making it more time sensitive as far as publication dates?

You need to know who your audience is. Who are you writing for? Will your readers be children, adults, men, or women? What age group? Are your readers white collar or blue collar or both? Are you writing for the urban or suburban population?

Finally, there is the title. Having a working title helps you to keep in line with the flow of your book. This title does not have to be etched in stone and can be changed later if you decide to change it. A good rule of thumb with titles is to do a basic title search on Amazon to see if the title is already being used.

Now turn to a blank piece of paper and answer the following questions to identify some of your goals for writing (There are no right or wrong answers. Just try to answer as honestly as you possibly can).

Write the questions and the answers in your notebook (or you can answer in the space provided if you prefer).

1. What type of book do you want to write?

2. What makes you an expert in this area, or why do you feel that you are qualified to write such a book?

3. What do you hope to achieve by writing this book (why do you want to write this book)?

4. When do you want your book to be published and made available to the public?

5. Who is your audience?

6. What is the title of your book?

As I mentioned before, there are no right or wrong answers. The reason that I asked you the previous questions is to help put your goals of writing and publishing your book into the proper perspective. In order for you to be successful at writing and publishing your book, it is important to identify your goals for writing a book before you start.

Take a few minutes now to expand on (if needed) and reflect on your answers to the questions in this chapter.

Power Point 2:

Setting goals helps you to get what you want to do done. In order for you to be successful at writing and publishing your book, it is important to identify your goals for writing a book before you start.

CHAPTER THREE

FOCUS (ON GETTING IT DONE)

In order to complete the process of writing your book, you must keep your focus. The answers to the questions in Chapter Two will help you to focus on what you are working to accomplish – or what your end-goal is. As with any goal, it is a good idea to write what you want to accomplish down and to go back on a regular (I recommend daily) basis to review your goals.

Reviewing your goals on a regular basis, will remind you of what you hope to accomplish and why. Now let's identify your why. Get out your writer's notebook or use the space below and answer the following question:

What is your why? I know this question is similar to question 3 in the last chapter, but I really want you to zero in on and be very specific and clear about your reason for writing your book. Is it for closure? To help someone else? To tell your story? To make an impact in your area of expertise? To motivate or inspire someone? Or maybe to use as a trade book for your business or ministry? (Write specifically why you want to write a book.)

What is your why?

It is very important for you to know your why for writing because, believe me, there will be moments when you clutch your head in your hands and ask yourself "Why?" You will begin to question why you are even bothering trying to write a book. That's why in the goals section, I mentioned that you need to pinpoint why you want to write a book. Take a minute to answer the above question in detail. What is your why? Why do you want to write a book?

If you are using a notebook, write the question and your answer down because you are going to need to come back to it during the times when that voice in your head tells you that it's no use or that you might as well quit.

Your reason why you are writing your book will stand up and answer back. Your reason why will keep you moving forward to successfully accomplish your goals of writing and publishing your book.

Without clear goals and focus, it is easy to forget why you are writing and why you want your book to be published and held in the hands of those who will read it. Once you forget your goals and purpose, it is even easier to get sidetracked or discouraged. At this point, there is a higher likelihood that your manuscript will end up in a desk drawer someplace or stuck on a flash drive or the hard drive of your computer.

There it will be left alone to die off in your memory. Only to be remembered from time to time, and even then, it will probably be pushed aside until you can find time to write. Which, I'm sad to say, in most cases, is never. I believe that won't be the case with you. I believe you'll be like me cranking out that first book and the second, and the third until all of the books inside of you are written.

I can't tell you how many books I have hanging in the balance waiting to be finished. What I can tell you is that I will work to finish each and every one of them because of my why. My why is to make a positive difference in the world and to empower others to live their purpose and live in victory every day. Every book that I write is written with my why pushing me.

In due season, I will write every book that I have started. I have a personal goal to write 100 books and I'm already over 60 years old, so I'd better get busy! Well, I digress. Back to you and your book.

You probably already know how easy it is to lose focus of your goal to write a book. Chances are, you already have a book that you've been working on. Chances are also that you have gotten stuck with your writing. Or perhaps you have simply been too busy to write. That's understandable. We know how busy life can get. There is so much to do and so little time to do it. Therefore, it's easy to get sidetracked, distracted, discouraged, and just plain stuck. It is for that reason that I have asked you to write your goals and your "why" down and focus on them on a regular basis.

18

It is my belief, and it has been proven in my life and in the lives of those whom I have coached through the process of writing their books, that regular focus on clearly written goals increases the possibility of those goals being met and the tasks associated with those goals being accomplished.

Have you ever seen someone start a business without a business plan? Well, I have. Businesses without a plan are doomed to fail or at the very least, fall short of making a profit. The business owners had the right idea, but never took the time to write down that idea and review it regularly. I love the biblical text that says, "write the vision and make it plain so that those who read it can run with it" (Habakkuk 2:2). I see this as a runner in a race running to cross the finish line with a scroll in his hand. Imagine what would happen if there were no finish line in sight and no scroll. That runner would be running aimlessly and empty-handed. That's what happens when we don't write down the vision for our books. We end up writing aimlessly with no finish line, and we come up empty handed.

Have you ever seen someone build a house without a blueprint? Blueprints help to build stronger foundations and ensure that the house is built properly within a certain time frame.

Have you ever seen someone run a business or their life without an appointment book or a calendar? An organized and focused person will not only write down all scheduled appointments, but this same person will review his or her appointment book or calendar every morning upon starting the day and every night before going to bed. Reviewing the appointment book or calendar helps that person to focus on what he or she needs to do that day or on any given day. Most successful people use a "Things To Do" list. They focus on their appointments and things to do daily.

Daily reviewing of written goals will sharpen your focus. A sharper focus will increase your productivity and, ultimately, your chances of success. Focusing on your goals will help you to see yourself achieving them.

Before you move on, I need you to see it! Think about writing your book. Visualize yourself doing it. See yourself typing your book.

Visualize your book being published. See yourself holding your published book in your hands. Think about what your cover will look like. Visualize the title on the cover. See your name on the cover. See yourself obtaining the purpose for which you have written your book. See yourself crossing that finish line of being a published author. Finally, see yourself sitting at a table signing copies of your book for people who are standing in line to talk to you and take pictures with you while they hold your newly published book in their hands!

As Billy Blanks says in his Taebo video, "Visualize it. You've got to visualize it!" You've got to see it! Focus! What you focus on will often become real in your life. That is why I am asking you to focus on your goals by thinking about them daily and actually seeing yourself accomplishing your goals.

Type or print clearly the following questions along with your answers onto a blank sheet of paper. Remember to come back and review the questions and answers every day. Reviewing your goals daily will help you to keep them fresh in your line of focus.

1. What is my why? (Rewrite the reason why do you want to write and publish your book?)

2. Why is it important to **see myself** achieving my goal of writing and publishing my book?

3. Are you willing to take some time every day to review your goals and see yourself achieving them?

4. List some of the things (barriers) that may prevent you from concentrating on your goals every day.

5. List some things you can do to overcome those barriers?

Now look at your list. The things that you listed for question #4 are distractions and/or barriers. Some of them may even be excuses. Only you know the difference.

If they fall into the category of being distractions or barriers, (this includes some of the things that you **must** do on a daily basis like work, cooking, spending time with your spouse, taking care of the children), then make it a point to set aside some time from your busy routine to focus on your goals. Make a schedule to work on your book and stick to it. Set an appointment on your calendar to work on your book and get it done!

If, however, you have listed excuses for why you can't focus daily on your goals, I ask you again to see yourself achieving these goals. Think of how happy and proud you will be to hold a copy of your very own book in your hands. Think of the lives that you will impact with your book. Think of the legacy that you will leave for your children and your grandchildren. Adjust your focus and then go ahead and draw a line through the excuses. Now, let's get on with the process of writing your book. In other words, "No Excuses. Just Do It!"

Power Point 3:

See it. Believe it. Achieve it! Think about writing your book. See yourself holding your published book in your hands. Visualize the title on the cover. See your name on the cover. See yourself crossing that finish line of being a published author.

CHAPTER FOUR

ACTIVITY (GETTING DOWN TO IT)

Now that we have covered your goals and focus as they pertain to your book, let's get moving with some action (or activity). Of all three (goals, focus and activity), your activity is what is going to make this thing happen. Goals get the wheels moving in the right direction. Focus takes you a step further. With clear focus, you are now thinking about how to get your book written and published, and you believe that you can and that you will publish your book. With activity, you are putting some feet to your faith and beginning to actively make your dream of being a published author become a reality.

Congratulations to you. If you have read this far, you are motivated enough to take the journey to become a published author. Please be cautioned before we move on that writing and publishing a book is more than just a nice idea. There is a lot of work involved, and you will be doing most of it. If you are serious about writing your book, let's move on to what you need to do to get your book written.

But just before we do that, here are a few more questions for you to answer. You know the drill. Get out your writer's notebook and write and answer the following questions (write the question and then answer it in your notebook, or continue to answer in this book if that's what you have been doing):

1. Are you ready to commit to writing your book and getting it published in spite of barriers and distractions?

2. Do you refuse to accept excuses or negative thinking that may interfere with this goal?

3. Will you stay with this goal until the very end, giving it no less than your best effort?

If your answer to the above three questions is yes, then you are ready to move on. I assure you that if you are committed to making your dream of being a published author come true, it will manifest. It will happen for you. I cannot promise you a bestseller, but I can assure you that holding the first copy of your book in your hands will be an experience unlike any other.

I can still remember publishing my very first book back in 2003 and how excited I was when the books arrived. I vividly remember opening one of the twenty-five boxes of books that were stacked up in my kitchen and taking out one of the books. I was so happy that I just jumped up and down, up and down shouting, "Oh my God! Look at this! It's my book! Oh my God!"

As the books began to sell, I had to reorder over and over again, and that book, *Nobody's Business*, along with my other books, is still selling. I am still shouting, "Oh my God! Look at this! It's my book! Oh my God!"

The feeling is wonderful. The level of satisfaction is awesome, and the sense of accomplishment is unmatchable. Now that I've shared my experience, I would like to see the same thing happen for you. So, let's get down to business and start writing your book.

In the following sections, I will outline some of the activities that will need to take place in order to ensure that you have a quality product to deliver to your reading audience.

CHAPTER FIVE

WRITING YOUR BOOK

There is no getting around it. If you want to write a book, you must take time out to sit down and write the book.

So many people get an idea to write a book, and the biggest reason that the book does not get written is that they do not take the time to sit down and write the book.

There are many reasons for why you haven't written or finished writing your book yet. Let's take a look at some of them:

1. You don't know how to write a book.

This is probably the number one reason. Dreams perish for lack of knowledge. That is why I applaud you for reading this book and getting the information you need to have your dream of writing a book come to life. Keep reading, and you will no longer have to worry about not knowing how to write a book. That's because in the next section, I am going to show you exactly what to do and how to do it.

2. **Fear.** Fear is right up there with not knowing how. Fear of the unknown or even fear of doing something like writing a book can immobilize you to the point where you do nothing. You must take control over fear and not allow fear to control you or your destiny. If you have a desire to write a book, you are destined to do it. Move forward despite the fear and write your book even if you have to do it afraid.

3. **No Time.** If you don't make time, you will not get it done. You must think of writing your book as something that is an important part of your life (because it is). You must schedule in time for writing. Make a daily appointment to sit down and

write and commit to keep your writing appointment every day. Make the appointment for at least 30 minutes. I recommend that you shoot for 60 minutes. You will be amazed that at the end of 30 to 60 days you will have written or almost finished writing your book.

4. **You're not a good writer.** This is an easy one, and I have good news! You don't have to be a good writer to write a book. You just have to have a good idea, story, or concept that you want to put in a book. Write freely without thinking of misspelled words or punctuation. You will not be graded on your manuscript like a paper in school. You *will* be graded on your book by reviews and ratings though. But you don't have to worry about that because after you finish writing your book, you will have it edited by a good editor, and they will take away all of your misspelled words and grammatical errors (or at least the majority of them. As I always tell my authors, there is no perfect book)!

5. **I don't know how to type.** The solution to this is that you can handwrite your book with a pen and notebook and have someone else type it for you, or you can record it into a voice recorder and have it transcribed.

As you can see, there is no valid reason for you not to write your book if you really want to do it. Don't allow lack of knowledge, or fear, or not having time, or not being good at writing, or not knowing how to type to stop you from writing your book. You can do this! '

In the next two chapters, I will give you some valuable insight into the book-writing process for writing your story and/or fiction and writing non-fiction. If you are writing a non-fiction book, you will probably be tempted to skip the section about writing your story and/or fiction. Don't do it! A lot of what I am going to tell you about writing a story (fiction or non-fiction) is going to be helpful to you as you write your non-fiction book. So, keep reading.

CHAPTER SIX

WRITING THE STORY (FICTION OR NON-FICTION)

What Is Your Story About?

Before you start to write, you must know what you want your story to be about. You don't need to know everything that will take place in between the pages of your book, but you must at least start with an idea of what story you want to tell your readers. Take a moment now to plot out your story by answering the following questions. Write the questions and answers in your notebook (or use the space in the book if you have already been doing that).

Note to Real-Life Story Writers and Fiction Writers: Whether you are writing fiction about characters you make up, a non-fictional book about something personal that has happened in your life, or telling someone else's story, you can use this outline).

1. Who is the main character?

2. What is going on or has happened in this person's life?

3. What is this person trying to accomplish or what need is this person trying to fulfill? What conflict, trauma, or problem is this person trying to solve or what has this person already faced and overcome?

4. What is preventing the person from accomplishing his or her objective or fulfilling the need? For the true-story writer: What was the person's biggest obstacle?

5. Who are some of the other key players (boyfriend, husband, wife, mother, father, boss, child, enemy, lover)?

6. Where do you want to start? (Not necessarily the beginning)

7. How do you want the story to end? If it's your
   story or someone else's story that you are
   writing, how does the story end?

The answers to these questions will give you a working outline of where you want your story to go. It is not etched in stone, especially if you are writing fiction, because fiction has a tendency to take on a life of its own. However, I used an outline similar to this one when I was writing "*Nobody's Business*" and found it to be helpful. I pretty much stayed on course, but there were at least three instances where my characters took over the story and created their own reality. (Reality in fiction? – As you will see, all writing wants to write itself, and the author's life often ends up in between the pages of his or her book whether the book is fiction or non-fiction.) Sometimes you will have to just let go and go with the flow.

Writing fiction can be a lot of fun. As I mentioned before, the key to writing a fiction novel or telling your life story, is to allow yourself to let go. In other words, don't take your role as the writer too seriously. You don't want to hold on too tightly to the characters in your book or try too hard to have a bestseller.

Before I started writing my first novel, *Nobody's Business* (which is loosely wrapped around parts of my real life), I was working on another book. I struggled with that book, partly because I didn't know what I was doing. All I knew was that I wanted to write a book. I didn't know how I was going to do it, but I was determined that I would. So, I sat down and started writing.

The experience was both unpleasant and humbling. Humbling because I realized that I didn't know what the heck I was doing! I felt like I needed to take a class or something to find out how to write a novel (I eventually did end up taking a class and reading a few books as well). Also, it was an unpleasant experience because I was holding on too tightly to my characters. I was like an overly strict parent. I refused to let my characters breathe, talk, walk, or act in any way that might embarrass me.

Can you imagine how boring that story became? In fiction, you must let your characters go! If they want to jump, let them jump. If they want to kidnap someone, or get drunk or jump off of a cliff, you've got to let them go. I don't care how much you want to save them, consider the fact that they may not want to be saved.

That's fiction. Like real life, it has to play itself out. If you are guilty of restraining your characters to save yourself from the chance of being embarrassed or because you wanted or felt like you needed to be in control, try letting them go. You will get much better results if your characters are free. You will find that your story has suddenly taken on a life of its own. At this point, you will only need to sit down and put your fingers to the keyboard. Your story will write itself if you utilize this tip in your writing.

Tip #1: Let your characters go. Let them be free. Your characters are alive, and they want to have a life of their own. Let each character develop fully and freely.

If you utilize this tip, your characters will be more real and you the author, will be rewarded with a story that you can be proud of.

The Formula for Telling Your Story

During my research after finding out that I really didn't know how to write a book, I found out that through my own trial and error that there is actually a formula for fiction that can also be used to write your personal life story.

The formula is that I use is:

Conflict + Action + Resolution = Story

Imagine that – a simple formula for writing fiction or for writing your own life story. Throw in some **showing** and **emotion,** and your story will come alive.

What exactly are Conflict, Action, Resolution, Showing and Emotion? Well, I'm glad you asked.

Conflict is when someone wants something or wants to accomplish something and there is something in the way stopping them from getting what they want. In other words, they have a problem.

Action is the drama that takes place during the story while your character or characters try to get what they want.

Resolution is the end of the conflict, and it is usually defined as victory or defeat for the main character.

Showing is when you develop scenes with action and dialogue mixed with some emotions instead of just writing a dead explanation of what happened.

Emotion is used best when your characters are allowed to feel everything that they are supposed to feel in response to what is happening to them in the story.

Look at this example:

Roberto told Ruthie that he was unhappy when he saw that she had left her clothes all over the bedroom floor again.

Ruthie tried to explain. He walked into the kitchen and got a beer. Then he sat on the couch and watched the television set, ignoring Ruthie. Ruthie just stood there crying. Roberto told her rudely to go away and to stop crying. After a minute, knowing it was no use, Ruthie walked out of the room. She was crying because she was very sad.

That's okay. But it's not
that interesting, is it?
Okay, now try this:

Roberto stood in the middle of the bedroom floor. He kicked a dress across the room, then turned and glared at Ruthie. "Why are these stupid clothes all over the place?" He kicked a shoe and then picked up a silk blouse and hurled it at Ruthie.

"I-I-I was la-late this morning." Ruthie's lower lip quivered in fear.

"Move out of my way! You make me sick." Roberto pushed past Ruthie who turned around and followed him out of the room.

"Why are you doing this?" she whimpered as they stopped in the kitchen. "You know what I've been through."

"Yeah, I know what you've been through!" Roberto yelled as he opened the fridge and took out a beer. "And I know that you need to grow up and stop crying all the time."

He pushed past her into the living room and plopped down on the couch. He waved the can of beer towards the bedroom and popped the lid.

"Now go clean up that mess."

Roberto reached over and picked up the remote control from the coffee table. Ignoring Ruthie, he flicked on the TV.

The Nets and the Pistons ran across the television screen, chasing each other for possession of the basketball.

Ruthie stood there sniffling with tears flowing down her face and snot running from her nose.

Roberto turned to look at her. His lips twisted as a look of sheer disgust covered his face. "Go on!" He took a long swig from the beer, wiped his mouth with the back of his hand and slouched back on the couch, turning his attention back to the game.

Ruthie opened her mouth to say something, but no words came out. She sighed and slumped her shoulders, standing there staring at Roberto who continued to ignore her. Finally, she lowered her head and headed to the bedroom with tears still flowing down her cheeks.

How's that? I hope that you found it to be a little more interesting than the first example. The difference between the two is that in the first one I was telling you about Roberto and Ruthie and the second example is where I actually took you to their home and made you a fly on the wall.

The interesting thing about writing stories (true or fictional) is this, if you can turn your audience into flies and allow them to sit on the walls in the lives of your characters, they will love your work.

Tip #2: Give your readers a "fly on the wall" experience. They will love you for it.

Another thing that you must do is allow your characters to feel all of the emotions that they are supposed to feel.

Look again at the first scenario and list in your notebook (or below) some of the emotions that you see the characters feeling. Not much there, right? Now take a look at the second scenario and write down the emotions that you see in that scene. What emotions did you experience while reading each scene?

Question #1: What emotions did you see Ruthie and Roberto experience in the first scenario?

Question #2: What were your emotions in reaction to the first scenario?

Question #3: What emotions did you see Ruthie and Roberto experience in the second scenario?

Question #4: What were your emotions in reaction to the second scenario?

Better than the emotions that you saw in the scenario, are the emotions that you actually felt while you were reading them. What did you feel when you read the first scene? The second? That's what I'm talking about. You were actually a "fly on the wall" in the home of Roberto and Ruthie, and you probably found yourself feeling angry with Roberto for the way he was treating

Ruthie. Chances are you even felt upset with Ruthie for allowing Roberto to treat her so badly, or maybe you just felt sorry for Ruthie. Whatever you felt, the point is that you felt something.

That's what good story telling is all about. Make your characters feel their emotions and make your readers feel some of their own emotions in reaction to what the characters are doing and feeling. If you do this correctly at a very early point in your book, you will create a bond with your readers and your characters that will last long after they finish reading your story. This is what will make you a successful author. This connection is what prompts readers to write and post 5-star reviews on Amazon. Great reviews will help you to sell more books.

Again, the key to writing good fiction or making your personal story more interesting is to follow the formula of:

Conflict + Action + Resolution = Story

Also, for a really good story you must **show instead of tell,** and you **must have characters who are real with real emotions.** Remember to let your characters make mistakes, splash in puddles, and have temper tantrums. It's okay. Not only is it okay, but it is absolutely necessary for your characters to engage in spontaneous activities if you want to write a story that sells.

Tip #3: Make your characters feel all of the emotions that they are supposed to feel in response to what is actually happening to them in the story.

Characters without feelings are lifeless. No one wants to read about a book full of lifeless characters. Share the emotions of your characters with your audience. The audience will be better able to relate to the characters if they know how they feel.

So, there you have it:

1. Conflict
2. Action
3. Showing

4. Emotion
5. Resolution

Make sure that you have the first four elements in every single chapter. You can never have enough conflict. You must allow things to get worse before they begin to get better. This is not always pretty, but for telling a good story, it is indeed necessary. No one wants to read about the lives of characters where everything is going great.

People want to see the struggle. They want to know that there is someone that can relate to in your book or someone who has a worse life then they do (albeit fiction or even your personal story), and they want to see the victory from the struggle (some even want to see the defeat of the bad guy or girl in the book). Ultimately, they want to know how it all ends up. So, don't forget your resolution. Whether your story ends in victory or defeat, your story must end, and the ending must be tied up with the beginning.

Did you get that? The ending is right there in the beginning. You have a character that wants something or wants to accomplish something. That is the beginning. Whether they get it or not is the ending. Simple. Right? Yes, it is simple, and you can do it if you only remember the next tip.

Tip #4: The end is in the beginning. You just can't tell it until the action is over.

As a matter of fact, you may not even know how the story will end until the action is over. When I was writing *Nobody's Business*, and *Daddy Love*, I had no idea how each story would unravel. My characters actually took over the story, and they were full of surprises. If this is how your story evolves, buckle your seatbelt. You are in for a great ride.

If you use the outline and the formula that I have given you, you are well on your way to writing a story worth reading. Revisit and review this information while you are writing your story to make sure that you stay on track. Don't forget to check each chapter for conflict. Every chapter and every scene should have some conflict until you get to the end of your story. Then let your story decide how the conflict will end.

Point of View

The next thing that I want to talk about is point of view. In every scene, choose the person whose thoughts you would like to reveal to your audience. It is important to remember not to jump in and out of your characters' heads sporadically while trying to show your readers what your characters are thinking. As a beginner, you want to pin it down to just one person per chapter or things could get confusing for your readers.

If you want to reveal the thoughts of more than one character, try doing it in different chapters and never with two characters at the same time. Some great writers have managed to do multiple points of view in the same chapter, but until you're ready and have mastered the "point of view" craft, try to stick to just one character in each chapter.

In my book, *Nobody's Business*, I told the whole story from Clara's point of view. Because they knew what she was thinking, my readers were able to totally identify with Clara and stay with her throughout her struggles in the story. This proved to be very effective for my first book. People are still asking me about Clara and what's going on with her now (as if she were a real person!) I used the same strategy in my second novel, *Daddy Love,* and I plan to use this strategy until I am comfortable working with more than one point of view at a time. As a matter of fact, I actually like using one point of view because it makes my story easier to follow.

When writing books, you want to make sure that you tell your story in a way that's easy to follow. Don't jump all over the place making the reader dizzy trying to figure out what is going on in your story. It's fine to switch scenes. Just make sure that you have smooth transitions between your scenes. There is nothing that will make a reader put a book down faster than confusion. Point of view helps you to stay within the structure of your story. Transition with your point-of-view character as if you are really living his or her life.

Tip #5: In order to make smooth transitions in your story, choose one point of view and stick with it. Don't take your readers into the head of too many characters. It can get too confusing.

CHAPTER SEVEN

WRITING NON-FICTION

Writing Non-Fiction That Delivers

Non-Fiction can be autobiography (also covered in previous chapter), self-help, how to, poetry, technical, or spiritual. Basically, there are no rules for poetry because it's a matter of expression. With an autobiography, it's your life and you have the freedom to tell the story any way you want to, although you still want to use the formula. With an autobiography, it should be easier since you already know the story. Again, as covered in the previous chapter, the formula for writing autobiographies is the same as writing fiction:

Conflict + Action + Resolution = Story

Don't to forget to add in the elements of **showing** and **emotion**. I would definitely advise you to try to keep the story as interesting as you can, or you will lose your readers. If you are writing an autobiography, or a book about somebody else's life, you can use the chapter on writing fiction to bring your book to life.

If you are writing a self-help, how to, or spiritual book, one of the most important things to identify is what you want to tell your readers. Once that is settled, go ahead and tell them.

You want to organize your material in such a way as to make sure that you are giving your readers as much information about your subject as they need in order for them to get the most out of your book.

If you are writing a book based on some information gained from research or experience, you want to keep in mind the question: "What's in it for me?" With most books, but especially self-help and spiritual, people want to know what they will gain by reading that particular book.

I find that even with reading fiction, people want to know what's in it for them (You'll find that the reason most people enjoy reading a good fiction book is that they can identify with the characters and the story, and they are inspired to make some decision or change). That is why it is important in all types of writing to develop a hook with a synopsis (back cover summary of the book's contents) that will let readers know what's in it for them. Do this before you write your book and make sure that you answer the question before the end of your book.

Answer The Question: What's in it for me?

Take a minute now and write down why I should read your book (In other words, "What's in it for me?).

Why should we read your book? WIIFM?

If you are using a notebook, write down the question and the answer in your notebook so that you can refer back to it while you are writing your book. This will help you to stay on purpose in your writing.

Tip #6: Make sure that you answer the question "What's in it for me?" when writing your book. Your readers will want to know why they should read your book. Write your book with the answer to that question in mind.

With most non-fiction books, you will need to do some research on your topic. Make sure that you give credit to all sources that you use in your book. You will need permission to use copyrighted information. You can reference that source, but make sure that you have permission before copying parts of someone else's work. There are guidelines and limitations as to how much of someone else's work you can use. Research and keep those limitations in mind as you write your book. Be diligent about not infringing upon other authors' copyrights. That way you will not set yourself up for a lawsuit by using someone else's material in your book without permission.

Copyright infringement can be costly and most importantly can be avoided with the next tip.

Tip #7: Learn the guidelines about using copyrighted material. When in doubt about what you can use from another author's book, contact the publisher or the author and ask for permission.

With self-help, how to, and spiritual books, the key is to identify a need and fill it. It also helps to choose a topic that you are interested in, preferably one that you are passionate about and have at least some knowledge of.

Once you have your topic, brainstorm all of the things that you already know about the topic. Then go ahead and do some research.

Writing Activity for Non-Fiction

Take a page in your writer's notebook or use the space below and do a brainstorming session. Write down all that you know about the topic you are writing about.

Then go ahead and add any other ideas that you have for your book and what you would like to add that you may not know a lot about but can get the information through research. Don't skip anything! Put everything that comes to your mind on that piece of paper or in the space below).

Finally, go over what you have written during your brainstorming session and put together a working outline by pulling out and listing all the things that you want to cover pertaining to your topic. This can also serve as a tentative table of contents.

List 5 to 10 things from your brainstorming session that you would like to write about in your book (this will serve as your tentative table of contents or your working outline for your book):

1.
2.
3.
4.
5.
6.
7.
8.
9.
10.

Now that you know what your chapters will be about, it's time to start writing your book.

You don't have to write the chapters in order. The important thing is to go ahead and start writing. Just write and write and write until you can't write anymore, and you will see you book begin to take form.

Tip #8: KISS – Keep It Simple Sweetie.

Keep your writing simple. Keep the language simple. Make sure that you cover your table of contents or your working outline completely. Remember not to worry about editing or making grammatical or spelling errors. Don't fret over punctuation. Just write. The editing and corrections will take place once your book is finished.

As I mentioned earlier, you don't have to write your book in order. You can pick a topic from your outline or tentative table of contents and write about that. Write on your topics as you are inspired to do so until all of the topics are covered.

After you finish writing, you can then go back and organize your manuscript so that it flows smoothly. Once that's done, review your manuscript to see if you have left anything out.

Or perhaps there's TMI – too much information. Go ahead and trim the fat, leaving in only the information that you feel will be useful. Don't take out too much, and make sure that your writing reflects your personality. In other words, make sure it has life. I usually write like I speak. That way my reader feels that I'm talking directly to them face to face. No technical terms (or very few), no fancy words, just the plain, simple, facts.

Let's Start Writing That Book Now If You Have Not Started Already

Congratulations! You have taken the time to learn about how to write your book! You have gained some valuable information and tips about the book writing process. This is a big first step, and I commend you for being serious enough about writing your book to get informed.

Now it's time for you to get up, go over to your computer, or grab your laptop and write!

You are one step closer to writing your book and becoming a published author. Don't worry about how to publish the book. The first part of this book was about getting you motivated to write, getting you to set goals, get focused, and get moving with some writing activity. My goal in this book was also to leave you more informed on how to write your book, where to start and how to successfully write your book.

Once your book is written, it is my hope that you will take the next step to get it published. For now, what I want you to do is write your book, but don't worry. In the next chapter, as a bonus, I have written some tips for publishing your book so you will know some of the steps you will need to take to get your book published.

Writing Exercise: Set the daily appointment in your calendar to spend time writing your book. In order to write the book, you must write every day. Just like you make appointments for other things and people, make appointments with yourself to write your book. Put **time to write** on your calendar daily and commit to keep writing until your book is complete.

Tip #9: Have some fun. Don't allow writing to be another job that stresses you out. If you feel yourself getting stressed out, back up, take a deep breath, and start all over again. Enjoy yourself!

Power Point 4

Breaking Through Writer's Block: If you get writer's block, remember your reason for writing your book. Remember your why and put yourself in remembrance of what you want to tell your readers. Look over your working table of contents, pick a topic or chapter and keep writing!

CHAPTER EIGHT

TIPS FOR PUBLISHING YOUR BOOK

O nce your book is finished, it's time to begin
to look at options for publishing your book.
There are many ways to publish your book. You
can self-publish, use a publishing services
company, or you can even opt to go the route of
traditional publishing. In this book, I wanted to
focus on getting you to write your book, but I
also want to give you a few tips on publishing, so
you have an idea of what you'll need to do to get
your book published and in the hands of your
readers:

Tips For Publishing Your Book

1. After your book is written, make sure you
   have it professionally edited.

2. Make sure to properly set up the interior pages of your book. You can use Word. You do not have to pay for expensive software. If you are not technically savvy or do not know how to lay out the interior of your book so that it looks professional, you will probably want to hire someone to do this for you. There are a lot of publishing services companies out there who can provide all of the services that you need to publish your book.

3. While your book is being edited, get your book's cover created professionally. Unless you are a graphic artist, do not attempt to do it yourself.

4. You will need an ISBN and Barcode for your book. Have your book copyrighted and listed in the Books In Print database. This will allow booksellers everywhere to find and order your book. You can find out more information on these items at www.bowker.com.

5. You do not have to pay thousands of dollars to have your book published. At Diligence

Publishing Company (and other publishing services companies), you can have your book published for a very reasonable and affordable price *and* buy author copies of your books at a low price. Low book prices for author copies is something you want to make sure of when shopping for a publishing company. Some companies will charge you to publish your book, and then charge you a surcharge to buy your own books from them. I have seen book prices as high as $9.00 - $10.00 for author copies. That is much too high and cuts too deep into the author's profit margin). Some companies will let you purchase the services you need a la carte You may need to purchase editing, interior text layout, cover design assistance and help with setting up your account and submitting your files online to the publishing platform or the printer of your choice.

6. You can self-publish on Barnes and Noble, LuLu, and Amazon KDP and Kindle for free. There is no charge when you set up your book on these platforms, however, they will take a percentage of your sales and pay you

royalties on each book that you sell. You can also publish in IngramSpark for a small setup fee. IngramSpark will distribute books for you, but they do not sell your book on their website like the other platforms. Even if you self-publish, it's a good idea to work with an established publishing company so that you can use their imprint which will give your book more credibility.

7. Do not give away the rights to your book. They are valuable, and if you write your personal life story or fiction, there is always a chance that you will be able to sell movie and play rights or even make your own movie or play based on your book. The sky's the limit.

8. These are just a few publishing tips to get you started in the right direction. Publishing a book is not easy, but when you have the right information, just like writing the book, it can be done. Also, keep in mind that you don't have to do it alone or reinvent the wheel. There are many companies out there that can help you to publish your book. You can find

more information about my publishing company at my website, www.dpc-books.com.

Finally, Remember This: Yes, you can! Yes, you can write a book! Yes, you can have that book published or even publish it yourself! Yes, you can! It's possible!

Tip #10: Don't stop writing! No matter how hard it may seem or how hard it gets, you have to believe this one thing. It's possible! It's possible for you to fulfill your dream of being a published author. It's possible for you to write your book. Don't quit. Don't stop writing. There is a book in you. It's time to get it out!

Final Note from The Author

I wrote this book to help you and other emerging authors to get started writing the book or books that you all have inside of you just waiting to get out. I hope you have found the information helpful and are motivated to write your book. If after you have read this far, you feel that you need help writing and/or publishing your book, I have resources available to you through my empowerment and publishing companies that can help you. For more information, visit my website www.rebeccasimmonsempowers.com and sign up for a free consultation.

You can do this! Thirteen books ago, I was right where you are. I wrote my first book and so can you. Happy writing!

ABOUT THE AUTHOR

Rebecca Simmons is a wife, mother, author of thirteen books, pastor, motivational speaker, empowerment facilitator and publisher. She has been writing and publishing books for herself and other authors since 2003. She has written and published 13 books of her own and helped many other authors to publish their books.

She is the CEO of Diligence Publishing Company and Destined for Victory Unlimited, Pastor of New Creation Christian Ministries, and founder of Woman to Woman Empowerment Group. Her purpose is to empower, inspire and motivate others to tap into their true identity, live in purpose and have total victory in every area of life. Part of that mandate is to help others to release the books that they have inside of them waiting to be written and published.

Her website is
www.rebeccaesimmonsempowers.com

OTHER BOOKS BY REBECCA SIMMONS

- ➢ *Nobody's Business*
- ➢ *Daddy Love*
- ➢ *Don't Die in The Wilderness*
- ➢ *Pump Up the Power: Get the Life You Want*
- ➢ *The Cry of a Woman's Heart: Healing the Pain of the Past, Traveling the Road to Victorious Living*
- ➢ *Making Marriage and Relationships Work*
- ➢ *MAN Problems: No More Broken Hearts*
- ➢ *You're Better Than That: Real Talk for Ladies Who Want God's Best*
- ➢ *Manifesting Kingdom: Unlocking God's Blessings and Abundance in Your Life*
- ➢ *God Is a Promise Keeper*
- ➢ *Moving Forward When Life Lets You Down*

Most books are available on Amazon or on the author's website:
www.rebeccasimmonsempowers.com